Cats as Cats Can

Tomi Ungerer

Tomi Ungerer

Cats as Cats Can

Tomico

A division of the Roberts Rinehart Publishing Group
Boulder • Dublin • London • Sydney

Copyright 1997 by Diogenes Verlag

International Standard Book Number 1-57098-160-4

Library of Congress Catalog Card Number 97-67691

Published in the United States and Canada by
TomiCo
The Roberts Rinehart Publishing Group
6309 Monarch Park Place
Niwot, Colorado 80503

Distributed to the trade by Publishers Group West

Published in Ireland by
TomiCo
Town House and Country House Publishers
Trinity House, Charleston Road
Ranelagh, Dublin 6

Published in England, Scotland and Wales by
TomiCo
Airlift Book Company
8 the Arena, Mollison Avenue, Enfield,
Middlesex, England

Published in Australia and New Zealand by
TomiCo

Peribo PTY Ltd.
58 Beaumont Road
Mount Kuring - GAI
NSW 2080 Australia

To Thérèse Willer

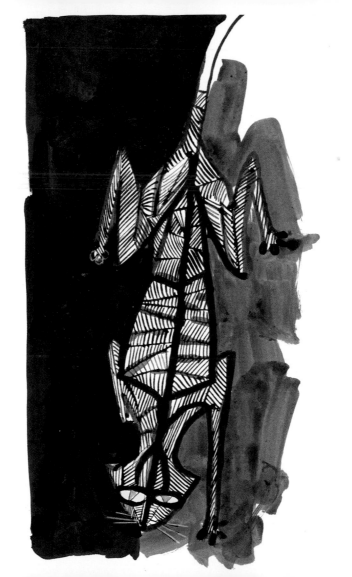

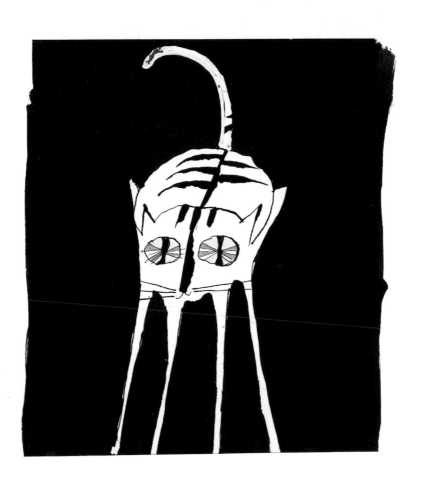

Tomi Ungerer

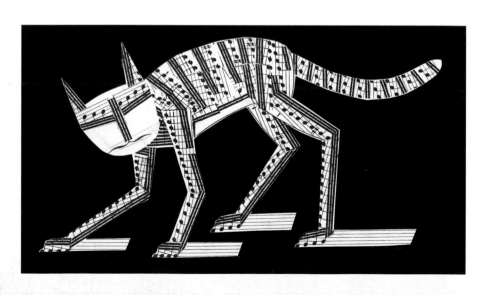

Riviera

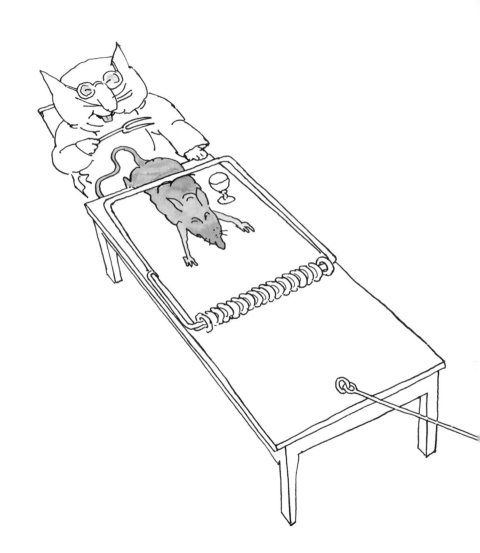

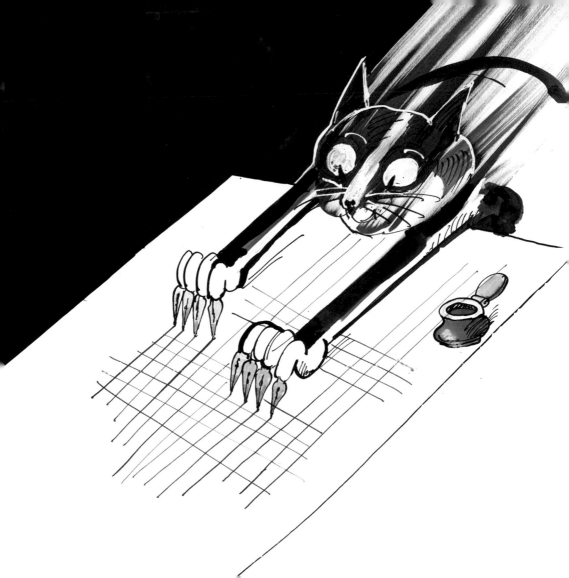

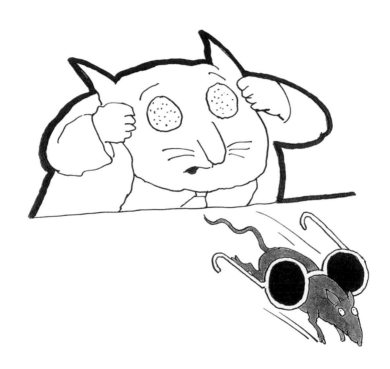

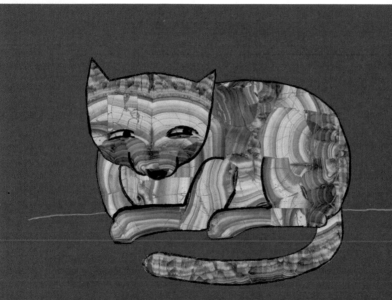

Malachit

Nova Scotia, Canada, 1973. Unafraid of the water, Piper leads the way.

I love to watch and draw animals, and cats are one of my favorite subjects. At rest or in motion, these languorous, slinky, sinuous and sensuous, wily and selfish creatures have been a constant source of inspiration throughout my life, and my observations of their behavior have resulted in hundreds of illustrations. Particularly important to me were our two beloved Burmese cats, Piper and Heidsieck, who lived with us in Canada in the 1970s. To this day they show up in my prints, advertisements, posters and books (Piper was my model for Toby in No Kiss for Mother).

In my book about my years in Canada, Far Out Isn't Far Enough (1983), I chronicled and illustrated some of the events in the lives of Piper and Heidsieck. The following excerpts from Far Out Isn't Far Enough, along with the many pictures in this book that they inspired, provide, I believe, both a fitting conclusion to Cats as Cats Can, and a tribute to their memory.

—Tomi Ungerer

Cats are clever, and they know it. Still, they can be fooled like anybody else. Between the kitchen and the entrance hall we have a glass door, which for a long time had a glass pane missing. The cats were in the habit of using this blank space as a passage. The day the new pane was mounted in its proper place was a day of great pain for our cats. They kept trying to hop through it but would crash against the glass. How we enjoyed their discomfiture, egging them on with cat-calls, sneers and cheers. *En francais on peut bien dire qu'ils sont tombres dans le panneau.* Ridiculed, they seem to have lost some of their feline cunning.

Heidsieck has been in pain lately. We take him to see a vet. The verdict is final: cancer of the bone. The cat has to be put to death.

A friend, depository of so many memories, has left us. There is a gaping hole in the texture of our life.

Heidsieck was a Burmese cat. I had bought him along with Piper, his younger half-brother, in New York for Yvonne when we met.

He was a very proud, class-conscious cat, who would never lower his standards to such menial tasks as hunting. He had the noble presence of a pharaoh's mummy, and looked as if he had just stepped out of a hieroglyph. We should have built a pyramid to his memory.

He would refuse to eat unless left in total privacy, though we once fooled him: I had fetched a fairly large piece of plastic pipe, in the middle of which we baited a very special dainty lunch of chopped meat. We placed Heidsieck at one end of the pipe and he crawled in to enjoy his meal in peace. Unbeknownst to him, we introduced Piper at the other end. The pipe suddenly shook and rolled convulsively echoing a duet of screeches. The cats, fighting with arched backs, could not easily back out of the pipe, and we finally managed to pull them out by their tails. For once, Heidsieck's pride emerged ruffled and tousled and badly in need of loving. He loved affection, and when he got the slightest caress he would literally melt like a piece of butter.

He would never hunt rats, mice, or birds. He made only one exception, for young bunny rabbits. He just could not resist the fun of catching these toy-like hoppers.

There was one very fast and clever survivor who took shelter under the wood pile, where the cat couldn't reach him. Yvonne named him Scooter. Well, Heidsieck did get him, in front of Yvonne's eyes. She cried and cried.

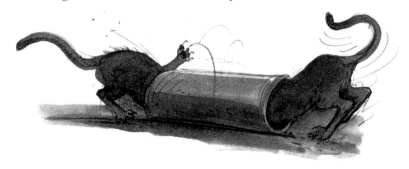

Piper, on the other hand, is a reckless rogue, unyielding to any form of affection except the dog's deviate performance already described.

He is a relentless hunter: out all day, out all night. No weather will stop him. He is the only cat I have ever seen fearless of water. Ornithologically, he is devastating. We have had a hard time keeping him inside; when we do he punishes us by urinating on the carpets. There was a time when every morning he would step out of the house and come back soon afterwards with a tern. To correct this bad habit we resorted to an old-fashioned trick, which consists in tying a dead bird around the cat's neck. A tern is a rather large bird. Piper carried it around for a whole day. He didn't seem to mind very much, and the following day we let him out, still dragging his victim on the ground. He was back half an hour later with a new victim in his jowls and the old one still tied around his neck. He looked like Josephine Baker at the Folies-Bergeres, in a display of feathers.

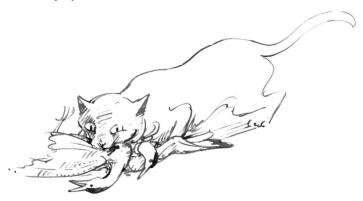

How Piper is able to catch these birds is a mystery; terns are aggressive. Sickle-winged, they will dive like stukas, aiming for the head of would-be predators. But in contrast to its bellicose behavior, the tern also stands out for its good manners: in courtship it will present its future partner with a fish, the way humans do with a bouquet of flowers.

Every night we lock up the barn. We take Piper along and drop him there to work on the rats. One night we snuck silently into the barn. We had it all planned. I would drop the cat inside a stall and Yvonne would flick on the light at the same moment. It worked perfectly. The scene that was given to us to witness was performed with wizardry:

Piper catching three rats in one flash. One with each paw, the third with his teeth.

Now that Heidsieck is gone, Piper's personality has changed overnight. He has become loving and lovable, stays home, and doesn't go out hunting anymore.

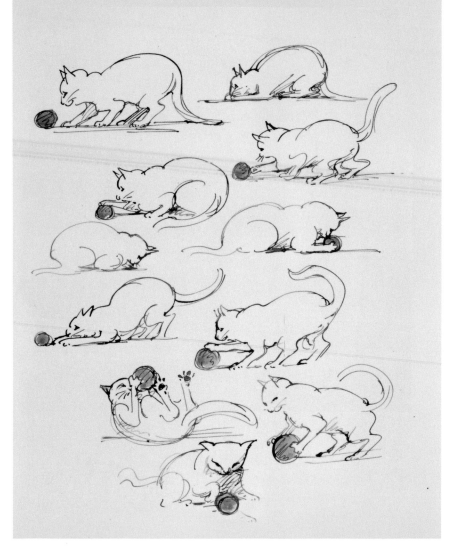